Reflection of Thoughts

Marius Alexandru

Published by Marius Alexandru, 2021.

While every precaution has been taken in the preparation of this book, the publisher assumes no responsibility for errors or omissions, or for damages resulting from the use of the information contained herein.

REFLECTION OF THOUGHTS

First edition. April 21, 2021.

Copyright © 2021 Marius Alexandru.

ISBN: 979-8224750832

Written by Marius Alexandru.

Table of Contents

"Poetry is a reflection of thoughts,
The writer's thoughts,
Reader's thoughts,
A mirror of ideas,
A portal to the imagination,
A breath of love, a flight, a dance..."

A New Creation

It's snowing
with snowflakes and stars,
with grace and purity
from God,
cleansing my soul,
-salvation-
washing my mind,
-metanoia-
changing my body,
-transcendence-
I became an incandescent bird
flying into the sun
the faith, the hope, the love
my three wings
make me special, unique,
maybe weird,
but I don't care,
I am a brand new me,
a new creation

A silent tear

A silent tear began to fly,
and the wind caressed all the olives tree,
The Son of God ready to die,
for all of us, for you and me.
Red drops of sweat
dripped on the garden's stone,
The price for our sin is set,
It's paid in full by Him alone.
A silent tear rose to the stars,
and it melted in the pure gleam,
Was hiding in it the mark of the nails, the scars,
The crown of thorns, the bloody stream.
A silent tear fell into the ground,
The trembling Earth felt the holy sacrifice,
I once was lost but now am found,
Amazing Grace, He paid the price.

Addicted to Love

I'm addicted to love's sweet sickness,
I'm a slave, but I can sing in heavy chains,
I'll never ask for your forgiveness,
My tears adore September's rains.
I'm sick, but what is my disease?
Misunderstood and left alone,
An old piano, with no fingers on the keys,
My words, my tongue turned into a stone.
I am a songbird scared by the birds of prey,
I sing my song without a word,
Why do you go, why can't you stay?
Why is my silence never heard?
I promise my love now to you,
You know the song that's in my heart,
Above the clouds, the skies are blue,
Don't wrench our stars apart.

Afflicted, but not crushed

When the storms of life are raging,
When the winds so angry roar,
I show no sign of tired or changing
I am the tall, strong lighthouse on the shore.
I do not care how mighty is the storm,
The night will always go away,
Inside my soul is peace, and warm,
Tomorrow is another day.
I am a rock, and I will never give up
on standing there, unmoved by the crashing waves,
I'll get the beating, hold the pains in my huge cup,
dreaming of all the future coral caves.
"I am afflicted, but not crushed,
perplex, but not driven to despair,
struck down, but not destroyed."
I have my doubts I have my fear,
But by His Grace, I sing and give another cheer!

All my worth is found in You

At the end of my short journey,
I want to measure all my worth,
Freed from all the ceaseless worry,
I want to see my footprints on this earth.
What did I build? What would remain?
What are the most important things?
What if my life was lived in vain?
What if I'll never grow my wings!?
What if it's all just dirt and dust,
What if my works are fog and smoke?
What if my golds will turn to rust?
What if my life was just a joke?
It could have been so if weren't You,
To come along in times of strife,
To wash my sins to make me new,
To give meaning to my life.
At the end of my short journey,
I trust Your words they're always true,
Covered by Your Grace and Mercy,
All my worth is found in You!

And if...

And if branches knock on the window, kind,
And the poplars slowly tremble,
It's that only to have you in my mind,
Close to my heart, close to my temple.
And if the stars kiss the lake, in evenings,
Magically illuminating its majestic bottom,
It's that only to make peace with my feelings,
Until it's all forgiven, all forgotten.
And if the darkest clouds are passing,
If the moon it's shining from above,
It's only to remind me all your laughing,
You're always in my heart, my love.

free translation "Si daca..." by Mihai Eminescu

Andrea Bocelli

The liberated light
The sound of wings in flight
A mystery for the angels
Comfort for the strangers
The unique, divine voice
Faithful rejoice
Tears of happiness
A touch of tenderness
Power in high notes
A melody that floats
Emotional drive
The joy to be alive
Finally made whole
Music for the soul
Beloved by so many
Incomparable Bocelli

April's Sonnet

Golden dust, the moon sifts musical notes,
I am once again on my knees grateful,
Praying with words in a poem that floats,
Waiting for the gorgeous month of April.
Little white snowdrops kiss the red sun's rays,
Green birds and butterflies dance in the breeze,
The silver stars sing endless, joyful praise,
It's new life in the murmur of the trees.
Happy tears turned into dew beneath feet,
God is always good, He's always faithful,
In every Spring, the earth grows perfumed, sweet,
I love the beautiful month of April.
Delicate flowers sing the violin,
Winter smiles as the Spring anew begin.

Autumn's Sonnet

The winds blow lightly in the silence,
It's raining with sad leaves in quiet tears,
Lost rays dream of light, hot impatience,
Upper tired branches slowly break their fears.
It's autumn. Hopes are dash in the dark fog,
Colors fade, and the pink flowers die,
The moonlight disappears in choking smog,
I began to roar I began to cry,
I choose to sing together with the wind,
To cry with the golden leaves through the rain,
To embrace a ray of light, to be kind,
To feel the great sadness and flower's pain.
It's autumn, from her wealth of hopes we reap,
A new time to laugh, a new time to weep.

Born Again-Haiku

a new day to shine
born again for a new life
metamorphosing

Born from The Ashes

The loyalty and love
shine through the cardinal's red feathers,
With its open wings,
the eagle shows us power, freedom, victory,
A bluebird tells us in a song
about the joy and hope,
and our happy future if we stay together,
We will be born from the ashes once again
as the phoenix into immortality.

Bring Peace, Tranquility, and Healing Once Again

If we could feel beyond the pain,
If we respond with love to hate,
If we could see the rainbow in the rain,
Our world will have a new great fate.
If we could see where we were wrong,
And in a whisper ask forgiveness,
Our world would be amazingly strong,
Full of compassion, loving-kindness.
If we could appreciate the Truth again,
Wipe away the tears of the sad ones
If we wouldn't compromise, wouldn't pretend,
If we wouldn't be throwing the first stones,
If we only knew how not to kill a dream,
And to smile at the stars night after night,
Peaches and apricots would bloom by the stream,
The larks would sing again in the light.
If we could, if we knew, but we are weak,
Because we can't, or we don't know-how,
Or we don't want to turn the other cheek,
We live only today, here and now.

Please God, break down the ugly walls,
And let the colorful butterflies fly,
Please listen to our desperate calls,
Don't let us too much longer in this lie.
Please wipe away our tears and stop our suffering,
Bring peace, tranquility, and healing once again,
Help us to bloom together in the new spring,

And in Your garden brothers to remain.

Burning Love

Inside this circle, this ring of fire,
my love for you is burning, eternal.
It flows abundantly like never stopping rivers,
like infinite waves,
like deep seas,
like boundless oceans.
The words are too small to describe my love for you.
I will always love you, my wife, my friend!

Butterfly-Septolet

incandescent wings
dancing into the new life
hope rebirth
transformation
change
mystery
beautiful butterfly

Butterfly-Haiku

incandescent wings
dancing into the new life
hope and love rebirth

Caught in Your Frosty Arms

Your heart is cold
like an iceberg from the North Pole,
Your touches, green-black mold,
reveals the darkness from your soul.
If you don't love me,
I don't care,
Darling, don't you see?
I love the stars from your blue hair.
You cut my heart,
Your eyes are like a knife that bites,
It's painful we must be apart,
But still, I love the northern lights.
Your big, white smiles
froze all my tears,
for miles and miles,
for years and years.
I'm like Titanic,
caught in your frosty arms,
But I love you, and I don't panic,
No "SOS" no loud alarms.
Will your heart ever melt?
Will you ever leave the oceans?
Will your love ever be felt?
Do you even have emotions?
I don't know,
and I don't care,
I love you I won't let go,
I kiss the stars from your blue hair.

Chicago, Winter at the Water Tower

I watched in awe,
bright, bright city lights,
I closed my eyes and started to dream,
I toured with angels the City Sights,
on the Chicago River, sailing down the stream.
With my eyes closed,
I felt the snowflakes
gentle touching my soul,
It was snowing silver stars, and white milkshakes,
The winter finally was taking its rightful toll.
The Water Tower,
like an old and magic castle,
stood there proving me that I'm alive,
An iconic symbol of the historic fire battle,
Few hundred feet from Lake Shore Drive.
I thought I saw Cinderella riding on a golden carriage,
But I was dreaming, or it was real?
It was a bride-to-be rehearsing for her marriage,
It's like I'm in a love story, at least that's how I feel.
It snows,
the joy is in the air,
I just woke up from my sweet dream,
Peacefully, by my window, I sit there and stare
at "Chicago, Winter at the Water Tower" a beautiful theme.

Christmas Memories

The sleigh bells are still ringing,
The Christmas tree lights are still shining,
God has blessed us with so many wonderful memories,
so many Christmases we shared in love.
Time is traveling so fast, but at Christmas, we stop a little bit
and dwell in its eternity.

Christmas Wish

I wish you at this Christmas to be full of shine,
have your glass full of blessings and happiness,
May that The Holy Baby Jesus places His Peace in your hearts,
and clothes you with Love and Light from the glories above.
Be always on the right path,
In the darkness of the night, be the Light,
To the earth be the Salt,
Be overwhelmed by Grace,
Smile and Joy be always on your face,
Let the whole world see and understand
that The Messiah was born in you!

Cloud Gate

Descending again from the cloudy sky
over the cold-eyed steel giants,
listening to the same old sad serenade,
the sorrowful flakes are dancing on the winding paths.
Winter's pale shrouds cover mysteries.
A huge frozen tear reigns lifeless in silence
like in an enchanted world.
Snows smoothly with semi-bright stars,
and confusing white angels,
on the streets that are ended in the lake.
Old memories fall apart.
I can barely remember it. It was a long time ago
when the snow was the greatest joy.
I stop on the street with no name that leads nowhere,
covered up in nostalgia.

Contest's Winner QAP 10X8

Winner of today's contest, who is he?
One of the greatest in all "allpoetry"
Tell me, why do you think he is so great?
His rhymes and poems I appreciate,
There is something special about his words?
With every line and verse, he struck love's chords,
Don't you think that you flatter him too much?
He's very humble, his pride out of touch.

"QAP 8X10" or "QAP 10X8", new forms created by Marius
Alexandru, on February 2021 consists of 4-5 stanzas of 2 lines each
stanza in a Question-Answer format.
QAP 8X10 form consists of 8 syllables each line with a total of 10
lines, respective 5 stanzas of 2 lines each.
QAP 10X8 form consists of 10 syllables each line with a total of 8
lines, respective 4 stanzas of 2 lines each.
It is a rhyming form with an AA BB CC DD EE rhyming scheme.
Both forms have 80 syllables, and are Question/Answer Style poems.
(first line the question second line the answer)
The name of the new form is "QAP" meaning Question Answer Poem.

Contrast (two palindromes)

cold stars crying, wilted flowers lying
candles burning, tears melting
dark nights, lost rights, rusted chains
blurry mornings broken wings
-desperation-
wings broken mornings blurry
chains rusted, rights lost, nights dark
melting tears, burning candles
lying flowers wilted, crying stars cold

....

roses red fresh, infinite tenderness
love eternal happiness, star shining
dreams restored, smiling sun
faith renewed, bluebirds singing
-expectation-
singing bluebirds, renewed faith
sun smiling, restored dreams
shining star, happiness eternal love
tenderness infinite, fresh red roses

Christ is alive! Christ has risen!

The old olive trees groan in the troubled garden,
The big drops of Love's blood pour down on the cold stone,
The sin's price was fully paid, the curtain... was forever torn.
"My soul is very sorrowful, even to death,"
"My Father, if it is possible, let this cup pass from me,"
the words come out with a heavy breath,
"Nevertheless, not my will, but Your Holy Will let it be."
One sad ray descends on His pale face,
In the celestial glories, all the angels are weeping,
On the Calvary's Hill, You took my place,
The heart of God for me is bleeding.
On the cross that unites heaven and earth,
Jesus hugged the whole world,
The Love blossomed to immortal mirth,
Instantly, the endless, amazing grace unfurled.
He died, He Who Was from the Beginning... The Word,
He prepared the white and clean clothes of the bride,
I'll always thank You for this, Lord,
I have peace and happiness by Your side.
Slowly the clouds dissipated in the skies,
The stone fell on the side, no more prison,
Christ is alive! Christ has risen!

Cursed Love

You stole my heart so many times,
There were no locks you couldn't break,
Then you repent from your sweet crimes,
And land again in all my rhymes,
Eternally awake.
Your lips and kisses make me tremble,
And then I'm left to die of thirst,
I'm just a pillar in your fire temple,
Our love was never easy, simple,
Our love is cursed.
Your eyes are lightening my life,
I'm left to slowly burn alive,
I've suffered enough grief and strife,
Your love cuts like a bloody knife,
A bold revive.
Your fresh, warm, perfumed breath,
It takes my breath away,
It makes me taste the height and depth,
I'll follow you happy through death,
My love, please, stay!

Dear Ana,

If I were a tear, I would happily
fully bathe in the ocean of love and hide in your pure eyes,
If I were a smile, I would merrily rest in the corner of your lips
never able to fly to others. If I were a hair from your chestnut hair, I
would tirelessly dance, kissing, from time to time, your velvety, white
cheek, If I were a drop of sun, I would paint you a rainbow on every
one of yours tears, and if I were a star, I would descend from
on high, to meet the light from your eyes. If I were a sea
wave, I would bring you pearls from the depths of the
sea, gemstones. If I were the breeze, I would
whisper lightly in the coolness
of the morning;
I love
you!

Disguised Angels-Haiku

crumbs of stars dancing
disguised angels- carolers
-music warmed my soul-

Don't give up on me so soon

Forever I will love you, dear,
So, don't give up on me so soon,
Virtue is not my forte point... that is clear,
Wait, please, at least 'til afternoon.
Let's time to pass, and let's forget,
Je t'aime, of course, I told you so,
So, don't do something you'll regret,
Please stay, please stay... don't go.
We are so good together, dear,
Wait one more hour, one more day, a week,
Let's see what will happen in a year,
God knows I want you as I speak.
Hide all your tears and... smile,
No more hurting, no more pain,
Return to me, let's reconcile,
For our love not to be in vain.
Gather all the memories we had,
Knockdown all the heavy walls,
Let's walk together and be glad,
Stay with me until the shadow falls.

Early Spring-Haiku

white snowdrops
kiss the red sun's rays
early Spring

End of October

The most beautiful Autumn of my life,
End of October, somewhere far away in my memory,
You came down from heaven like a ray of light, like a star,
and you have placed in my soul a new unique love.
It was something special that I didn't know before,
A feeling I cannot describe,
It was a different love, the father's love,
Something I just dreamed about in my boldest fantasy.
Whispers of angels were your crying sounds,
Every smile was like broken from Paradise,
I saw the sunrise in your shining eyes,
My heart's love, I promised you forever.
The first words you uttered with such cuteness,
I will keep them forever framed in my soul,
The most beautiful song in the universe,
The most expensive gemstones.
And, later when I let go of your hand,
You took the first steps. I was without breath.
You were as a Fairy from the most beautiful stories,
dancing like an angel in a heavenly play.
The sand in the hourglass runs way too fast,
I'm thanking God for sending you in my way,
You are my angel, my life,
You will be forever, my little girl.
You are and always will be a blessing for us,
Your mom and I will love you forever,
And If we could, we would bring the time back to be one more time
that beautiful day, the blessed morning, end of October.

Eternitarian (Palindrome)

dancing snowflakes and light create fairies and angels
purified wings flying faith and love
heaven reaching souls touching
hope renewed belief
magic eternal life
-immortal-
life eternal magic
belief renewed hope
touching souls reaching heaven
love and faith flying wings purified
angels and fairies create light and snowflakes dancing

Fall is Born in Poetry

Fall is born in poetry,
A new muse for everyone,
The leaves fall through golden verses
in rhythm and symmetry,
Enchanted rhymes on the run.
Fall is born in songs,
Springs tremble in choirs,
A gracious melody whose
sound loves and longs,
The wings of the wind, seraphic fires.
Fall is born in a dance of joy,
The tango of a full life,
Grace after grace in every step,
Memories of a girl kissing a boy,
In the fateful autumn,
now husband and wife.
Fall is born in aspirations, in dreams,
In smiles, in tears, in love,
The splendid autumn surround us,
In our souls flow steady streams
rising to the stars above.

Fata Morgana

I caught her, with my bare hands,
after years and years of searching,
Like a shadow in the glimmering sands,
She was waiting for me, lost and lurking,
I let her go away again,
with all my hopes, and all my dreams,
She disappeared in a gentle rain,
In drops of light, in sunny gleams.
Later I saw her in the ocean,
She waved at me, and called my name,
filling my soul with pure emotion,
But soon she changed in a small, blue flame,
It's maybe time for giving up,
To start to live life to its fullest,
To drink new wine from the old cup,
Without no fear against love's bullets.
I will renounce pain's camouflage,
Freely I'll fly to new horizons
I'll stop chasing the false mirage,
The night has passed, the sun is rising.

Fear

Fear
Fighting souls
Freezing the heart
Flighting away from problems
Faith conquers all the fear

Fears

With my soul covered by leaves,
I rest in the alley of remembrance,
Longing for the honey on your lips,
Longing for the tender whisper of love.
I'm afraid there will be no more flowers,
I'm afraid I will lose you in the rusty autumn,
I'm afraid you'll hide in the clouds,
And my heart will remain forever empty.
I'm afraid you will get lost among strangers,
Or you'll be born again, far away in other spring,
I'm afraid you will give yourself to the pine forests,
and you will let the wind lure you with his pleasant breezes.
Oh, please stay, stay with me in the new fall,
Covered with leaves to love each other,
Hugged, together like two drops of dew,
Let's kiss the ground and then melt in infinite.

Forever One

At the edge of the abyss,
I sit alone dreaming of you,
I remember your touch, your kiss,
And the sweet love that we once knew.
I can feel you in raindrops and rainbows,
Our souls dimmed stars by dawning light,
are wandering in the shadows,
out of the stranger's sight.
Dying a little bit each day I fully live,
Together, we we'll melt in the rising sun,
On the love's altar, my life as a sacrifice I'll happily give
for our souls to be forever One.

Grateful

Grateful for being with me through the storms,
and for the rainbow in your smile,
Grateful for the sunny mornings,
and for the shine in your eyes,
Grateful for the beautiful nights,
and for all the stars in your hair,
Grateful for the rain in your tears,
and for the thunder in your laughter.
I thank God every day for you, my love.

Hallelujah, Hallelujah, Christ has Risen!

Take light from The Holy Light,
resounds in the night,
Freed, happy souls sing,
The hope is reborn and the bells ring,
Hallelujah, Hallelujah, Christ has Risen!
Through the crack of old stained glasses
The Light penetrates,
Broken, has spread in millions of stars,
The almonds bloomed again in the garden,
Hallelujah, Hallelujah, Christ has Risen!
With the soul touched by Grace, by The Light,
I receive immortality,
His sacrifice on the cross forever transformed me,
Death is defeated, my life is full of Love,
Hallelujah, Hallelujah, Christ has Risen!

Happiest man among men

Dulled by the half-light of the distant stars,
My hope of love started to fade,
Injured by lost love scars,
I stand forsaken in the shade.
A hint of blue dissolving into her beautiful eyes,
was all I needed for my dreams to be reborn,
Soon I forgot all pains, all lies,
I woke up happy in that glorious morn
Redemption is never easy, is never simple,
Regaining trust is always very hard,
But when you see the heavens smile and twinkle,
You know that love is in your card.
When a dreamer climbs that way to touch the sun,
When all the hopes are rekindled once again,
It's a new day the love has won,
I am the happiest man among men.

Happiness (palindrome)

dreams of streams
full of love,
hope revived,
liberty in flying birds
and blue skies,
breathing hearth,
me inside happiness,
and,
happiness inside me,
hearth breathing,
skies blue and
birds flying in liberty,
revived hope,
love of full
streams of dreams

Happiness

I look in the mirror,
and I see your smile,
which you planted in my heart
many, many years ago.
I smile back and go to bed,
happy that you are there
sleeping peacefully,
dreaming of blue butterflies
and shining stars.
I hold you in my arms
and I promise myself
that I will never let you go.

Happy Birthday, my Sister

So many longing songs remain unsung,
but is still time and life goes on,
My sister, you are yet so young,
A light of hope at the break of dawn.
You conquered many mountains peaks,
With Love's music, you still sing along,
With compassion's water, you filled many creeks,
Your life is a sweet dance, a joyful song.
September's memories are now reborn,
So many night stories remain untold,
but is still time, no blowing horn,
Your soul is young, brave, and bold.
So many unquenchable tears of joy and pain,
So many dreams still to be dreamed,
So many dances in the rain,
So much time left to be redeemed.
May your song always be sung,
And be blessed in all you do,
May you stay forever young,
Happy Birthday, now to you!

Healthy and Cute (Limerick)

after he happily took the vaccine
turned into a zombie, yellow and green
but now he's healthy and cute
a strong and handsome new brute
his experience uncommonly keen

I am a mighty King

Walking quietly through this valley,
One might think that I'm alone,
Don't you see that I am happy?
I drank water from The Stone.
When the storms of life are roaring,
One might think that I am lost,
But I kept my brightness soaring,
Many oceans I have crossed.
So, don't count me out so soon,
I'm still molded, by The Potter,
Don't count me as out of tune,
He can make wine out of water.
When I'm sailing, angry, dangerous seas,
When the fear is all around,
When I'm deep down on my knees,
I still know I'm heaven bound.
I live my life without regret,
I sing, I dance, I laugh, I love,
So, don't count me out just yet,
Someone it's watching over me, from high above.
You haven't seen the last of me,
I blossom more and more each spring,
You haven't seen who I will be,
I am eternal I'm a mighty King.

I am Happy!

Golden dust of the moon sifts musical notes,
Blue butterflies are dancing in the sky,
It snows upside down with white snowdrops kissing the sun,
Silky flakes sing, the silver bells ring,
Tears of joy turned into dew on the still unborn grass beneath my feet.
I am happy!

I am Yours, and You are Mine

I am yours, and you are mine,
I'll never let you go,
I will drink from love's cup wine,
I'll never say No,
Our love will never cease,
I'll love you through death,
I will be down to my knees,
Breathing through your breath,
I am yours, and you are mine,
Together with one heart,
We will walk the love's red line,
We'll never be apart,
All I wished for I found in you,
My treasure, and my gem,
All my hopeful dreams come true,
My jewel, my diadem.
I am yours, and you are mine,
Throughout eternity,
Our love will brightly shine,
Cosmic infinity.

I believe

I believe in spring, I believe in the future,
I believe in you, and I believe in myself,
I still believe in us.
I believe in blossoming buds of love,
I believe in the sunrise that reflects your smile,
and in the sunset that hides your tears.
I believe in rivers that carry your shadows,
and in the forests that sings your longing,
I believe in the mountains, in your power, and your strength.
I believe in the breeze that gently touches your hair,
I believe in the stars that kiss your lips,
I believe in freedom.
I believe in flowers, I believe in music,
I believe in colors,
I believe in poetry.
I believe in forgiveness,
I believe in life,
I believe in the resurrection.
I believe in the rainbow after any storm,
and in the day after any night,
I don't believe in hate,
I don't believe in the lie,
I believe in the truth.

I Did Not Die-Sonnet

It's not a time to weep and mourn,
I hear so loud and clear the gong,
I have to go it is my turn,
Among the stars, I'll wear my song.
Why should your heart be broken sad?
I walk with God on golden streets,
I'm here with friends with mom and dad,
I sit with kings on royal seats.
I was not swallowed by the earth,
It's not a time for tears, don't cry,
I experienced the new birth,
I am alive, I did not die.
It's not adieu it's just goodbye,
We'll meet again, I did not die!

I Dream of a New Land

my soul chained with fears
caged in a dark place
cries with sorrowful tears
down my pale, hollow face
the notes of my song die
before even being born
my broken wings cannot fly
deep in my heart, I can feel
this sharp, constant thorn
I dream of a new land
the land of the blue skies
-the land of the free-
across this desert,
across this dry sand
across this stormy sea
will I dare to act on my dreams?
will I dare to rise and break my chains?
will I dare to free all the inside screams?
will I dare to reveal all my pains?
my soul without any fears
flies free in a colorful place
cries with new happy tears
down my bright, beautiful face
a new song is born in an instant
I carry it on my new silver wings
there's no time and no distance
I'm born in the eternal existence
my heart forever sings
I dream of a new land
the land of the blue skies

-the land of the free-
across this desert,
across this dry sand
across this stormy sea

I Gave You My Heart

I wanted to give you the poppies field
and the stars, the blue vault,
but full of love, shy, and clumsy,
I gave you a rose in a jar instead.
I wanted to give you precious stones,
beautiful pearls,
but full of love, quiet, in the evening,
I gave you only warm kisses instead.
I wanted to give you the trees and the forest,
and wings to ascend to the wonderful sky,
but full of love when we walked wandering the streets,
I took your hand instead and never let it go.
I wanted to give you waters, springs,
hills and mountains and the rainbow,
but full of love - on a holy day,
I gave you my heart and the key of its lock.

I Let My Soul Sing

I was playing with some words,
In my native Romanian Language,
I heard singing golden birds,
I knew I'm at a disadvantage.
How to make my words a song?
How to make the verses fly?
How to make my statements strong?
How to make peoples cry?
How to put laughter in rhyme,
Or the rainbow in my paper?
How to put a stop to time?
How will I describe a vapor?
I closed my eyes and dreamt,
and I let my soul sing,
touched by the angel sent.
He got me under his wing.
I learned that the sun can smile,
and about the talking sea,
I learned about the rhythm and style,
I discovered poetry.
I learned that rain means sorrow,
or new life, or grace and blessings,
White snowdrops could mean tomorrow
I learned how the choir sings.
Years, decades have passed by,
A few books, thousands of poems,
My angel watches from the sky
to his special, favorite poet.

I love You Too (Limerick)

When years ago, I told her, I love you,
I remember seeing green, black, and blue,
In my stomach butterflies,
When I looked into her eyes
I fainted when she said; I love you too.

I Need YOU

Every night I dream your kisses,
Your gentle touches and your sweet perfume,
Last summer's endless, silent blisses,
Your magic eyes, your youthful bloom.
I can feel your hand in my ruffled hair,
The love that's coming from your moving lips,
Do you want that love with me to share,
and to sail forever in eternal ships?
We will melt together in the sunset,
And will rise again in every morning,
We'll go so far as far we'll get,
Our love will be a fire burning.
There's something about you that I know I need,
Maybe your smile or your gentle soul,
Don't make my heart again bleed,
My love for you is beyond my control.
There's something about you that I know I need, I do,
This is a new feeling that I never knew before,
I got it now, I know that what I need is YOU,
Just YOU and YOU, more and more and more...

I rediscovered Love and Poetry

I close my eyes and dream,
and I listen to my soul singing,
surrounded by the angelic gleam,
and millions of silver bells ringing.
I learn that stars can smile,
and snowflakes know sacred mysteries,
I sit there happy in the snow awhile,
savoring my small victories.
I learn that snow is grace and blessings,
That The Light is The Life and The Hope that molded me,
I understand why my spirit writes and sings,
I rediscovered Love and poetry!

I stained my soul with white

Disguised as snowflakes, white angels descend smoothly from a
distant land.
It snows blessings, crumbs of stars
over my house, and my dreams.
Full of happiness, I stained my soul with white, and brilliance, and
warmth.
It was frozen, so I let it burn in love.
Eventually, it melted and flew out the window,
free to eternity, magnificent bird.

I started to Fly

I made myself wings from Faith and Love,
I was overwhelmed with longing from the heavens
forgetting right away, any pain,
I clothed myself in stars,
and I started to fly.
I made myself wings from Mercy and Grace,
Listening to the angel's choirs
I was surrounded by fire, by eternity's flame,
and instantly I forgot all the hard and bitter,
I clothed myself in the Sun,
and I started to fly.
I made myself wings from Assurance and Hope,
I felt like a snowflake, freed from any chains, dancing
full of peace, safe...
I understood that there is no time nor distance,
and free from me
I started to fly.

I want to feel

I'll give up all my gold and silver,
to touch a rose, to feel its beauty,
to hear the music of that crystal river,
to see the evening's sunset fiery ruby,
to barefoot walk-through evergreen, emerald grass,
how you radiate through the love's quartz prisms, I want to see,
how you are even more beautiful in the years that pass,
I want to touch, I want to hear, I want to see!
I want to feel the beeswax from your lipstick,
to taste your kisses, sweet like butterscotch,
to sip your love and get drunk quick,
to look in your sapphire eyes, to sit there happy, cry, and watch.
Our love, an unending diameter an unfading garland,
like an eternal white tinsel snowflake,
a daily kiss to all the flowers from our garden,
I want to touch, I want to hear, I want to see! I want to stay awake!
Our time on Earth has slowly gone,
we had our laughter, our smiles, our tears,
we'll soon wake up at the break of dawn,
and start to live for millions of years.

I'll fly away (QAP 8X10)

Why is the sky so blue today?
Because the clouds went far away.
Why is my love unanswered yet?
Because my love I never met.
When will my life be changed for good?
When you will leave this neighborhood.
What is the greatest thing you'll miss?
Without a doubt will be your kiss.
Will you return to save the love?
I'll fly away free like a dove.

"QAP 8X10" or "QAP 10X8", new forms created by Marius Alexandru, on February 2021 consists of 4-5 stanzas of 2 lines each stanza in a Question-Answer format.

QAP 8X10 form consists of 8 syllables each line with a total of 10 lines, respective 5 stanzas of 2 lines each.

QAP 10X8 form consists of 10 syllables each line with a total of 8 lines, respective 4 stanzas of 2 lines each.

It is a rhyming form with an AA BB CC DD EE rhyming scheme.

Both forms have 80 syllables, and are Question/Answer Style poems.

(first line the question second line the answer)

The name of the new form is "QAP" meaning Question Answer Poem.

I Will Let You Have Your Freedom

I caress your black hair,
I treasure your white skin,
To touch you I don't dare,
I marvel at your chin.
Indulge my eyes to cry,
Allow my ear to listen,
Quit chasing the dark sky,
Let my voices gleam and glisten.
No matter what I feel,
I will let you have your freedom,
My love for you is genuinely real,
Fiery sparkles in the new season!

Immortality-Haiku

born from the ashes
walking into the great light
immortality

In the Shadow of Your Wings

There's a place where safety resides,
Where I can hide from all my enemies,
There's a place where The Father gracefully provides,
Where I can hear Victor's melody.
There's a place where any scar is healed,
And all my tears are wiped away,
There's a place where my soul with peace is filled,
A place where I would always happily stay.
To that place, I often run,
I lay down my fears and woes,
I enjoy the rising sun,
And my new white as snow clothes.
In the shadow of Your wings,
The safest place I have known,
Beside the still waters and the cooling springs,
In the shadow of Your wings, never alone.
When the storms of life are coming,
When the winds so angry roar,
When I feel my world is crashing,
I dream of that Golden Shore.

Inside your scars

Inside your scars grows a new flower,
After a miserable long pitch-dark night,
After the cruel betrayal hour,
Bright colors glisten in the new morning light.
Your wound itches hurt and bleed,
But from your scarring and tears, and pains,
Will magically grow love's eternal seed,
and bloom white flowers in spring's rains.
The countless bruises make you stronger,
Through this temporary hardship,
you learned perseverance, endurance, patience,
Just wait, my friend, a little longer,
You soon will shine in His glorious presence.

It has to start with all of us

We want them all to see our Lord,
We want our land to be healed again,
But can we put down our sword?
Can we pour down love like rain?
We want the world to see our God,
To hear His Voice, to trust His Word,
We cry and cry from deeps untrod,
But into dark paths, we are hurled.
We know the plans He has for us,
But are we ready to begin?
There is no time left to discuss,
Why we still like to play with sin?
Give us the power, the first love,
Don't let us be asleep, lukewarm,
Watch over us from high above,
And make us towers, in the storm.
It has to start right here, right now,
With all of us with me and you,
You live in us, You'll show us how,
Give us the strength Your will to do!

It Is Raining with Cold, Rusty Leaves

It is raining with cold, rusty leaves
over my autumnal body and my tired temple.
I'm cold. Cover my unfulfilled thoughts and dreams
with Your Divine Grace and Your beloved Whisper.
The golden dust of the moon shakes easily
over my sad face and the leaden world.
I'm afraid. Make me wings, paint them in gold, and teach me to fly
to blue horizons and the glories of joy.
Stars fall one by one, one by one,
and they melt in the night of my dry soul.
I'm thirsty. Pour Love into my heart and mind,
and make me a fountain of living water.
Blond lights bathe in the dark,
In the corners of locked rooms, there are fights in prayer,
I long, I miss Your enchanting Face,
I miss the sound of the trumpet I miss You to come to gather us.

It Rains on People with Angels and Flowers

Today, the sky made its wings out of the clouds,
and it rains on people with angels and flowers,
The sun is red, like a clumsy child,
and the field is filled with poppy flowers.
A ray, wanting to be chicer,
discreetly associates with a daisy,
both thought the same thing;
to be tiaras for those on earth.
The trees are dressed in green,
The wind blows a ballad for the panpipes,
The birds gather in a choir and chirp a joyful song,
It's spring, and I'm happy!
I dance with the stars every night,
I'm dreaming of Eternal Spring,
A drop of Heaven smoothly dripped into my soul,
Ah, how beautiful the month of May is!

Je T'aime, Paris, Tu es ma vie

I dream of you each day and night,
La Tour Eiffel and its great height,
The lovers, kissing in your parks,
The magic stars, the flying sparks.
I see the city wrapped in light,
I am amazed by this rare sight,
I smell the coffee and croissants,
The pleasant aroma from your chic restaurants.
What a special matinee,
watching the tourists on The Champs-Élysées,
L'Arc de Triomphe and those who fought for France,
La Seine and its majestic, ancient dance.
The painters trying to catch a charming glimpse of you
Je T'aime, Paris... romantic view,
Je T'aime, Paris... you know I do.
Je T'aime, Paris, Tu es ma vie.

Keep the Smile-Haiku

after any storm
a new rainbow will appear
always keep the smile

Kiss My Sad Forehead with Love

Touch me with Your divine comfort,
like the gentle wind blowing at dawn,
And pour in me drops of Grace and Light,
Caress me with holy songs.
Kiss my sad forehead with love,
how the sun kisses the snowdrop every day,
Dress me in perfume and radiance,
and may that heaven be mirrored in my face.
Make Your Holy Spirit pours out on me,
Like a pure spring of living water,
Like a fountain full of the Word,
what flows over our old earth.
Flood my soul in peace,
And make it jump like lambs on the pasture,
In the holy hour beside the brethren to play,
To cry and laugh in the poetry's verse.

Let your soul sink in

I have a pad and pen
where to start, where to end?
Just pick it up,
and begin.
Let your soul sink in,
Let the words freely fly,
write with passion, touch the sky.
Write with red, the color of love,
write for the angels from above.
Close your eyes, imagine things,
let your thoughts grow special wings.
You have a pad and pen
where to start, where to end?
Just pick it up,
and begin.
Let your soul sink in,
Let your soul sink in!

Longing for the Blue Sky

The trees bored of so much yellow,
abandon their leaves thinking of springtime.
The springs dream of greenery and flowers,
and the sun cries sickly under the blanket of clouds.
On the path of rust, the light has withered and is in tears.
A butterfly stripped of his shadow is silently dancing.
Leaden sadness, old-fashioned melancholy lies on our faces
and we long for our youth.
A star is resting on a corner of the sky,
nesting in the tops of the tall, old pine trees.
On the mountains whitened by time, on the heights, on the ridges,
a black goat sinks into the snow.
A wild quince tree fills with optimism the earth,
spreading all-around a new air of gratitude.
Once again, a new song is born in all the cold hearts
and a longing for the blue sky and immortality.

Look Through It

When the fog of pain and doubt is raising
look through it with the eyes of faith
to see the great things you already have seen
and are there waiting for you; His Peace, Love, and Care.

Love at First Sight

Her smile struck a chord in me,
A song of Hallelujah was instantly born.
Love at first sight!

Love's Sillage

Your dance is majestic.
How an eagle glides through the sky,
in the same way, you float with your barefoot
barely touching the grass.
I follow the trail of the sound of your voice
how a ship navigates the ocean, lost in the storm
guided only by the light from your bright eyes.
A breath of your love fills my tired lungs,
You let yourself be inhaled in one pleasant smell,
I am alive. I can feel the scent of the ocean's breeze,
All I have to do is breathe.
A strong perfume like a powerful cocktail of memories
invade the old room, an aphrodisiac fragrance.
I inhaled into my soul this exquisite aroma,
and I exhaled my eternal love to you.
Over the sad piano
hangs in a frame your beautiful picture,
In the air still lingers your divine flavor
as a bouquet of fresh roses.
Everything around gives off your scent,
even the stillness.
I miss you so much.

Love's Tango

We wrap ourself lightly in the Fall
my love, my beautiful lady
Rusty and golden leaves fall
on our silver and tired temples.
So many rustles hide under our barefoot walk,
So many prayers we had, down in the valleys or on mountains top,
We left so many traces in the stars, in the sun, through storms, through rains,
So many wonderful seasons have passed, beautiful lady over us.
We shared the burdens and the joy,
The glass, the spoon, and the plate,
We also shared wounds, tears, and pains,
Failures and successes, smiles, and sweet pleasures.
It's raining slowly with huge splashes that urge us to dance, my beautiful lady,
I kiss a tear that's running down your soft white cheeks,
and we continue, as it is written for us, the tango of love in two.

Love

I gave my heart to a poem, and she dyed it blue,
then wrote with big red letters on the sky, I love you.
I gave my heart to a song, and she turned it into a romantic symphony.
I gave my heart to you. You gave back yours. Love.

Love's Sonnet

What is love, and how should I describe it?
A smile, a heart that beats only for me,
A flickering star in your eyes, that lit,
Blue sky, a high mountain, the deepest sea.
Winds that gently carries all your whispers,
Flowers that smell like your breath in mornings,
The cold spring's rain giving me soft shivers,
The freedom of the soul, spreading its wings.
The rising sun that caresses your hair,
The rain that mingles with your happy tears,
The breath of life, the water, and the air,
Blissful seconds, hours, decades, hundred years.
My love for you will never cease nor die,
"Would none had ever loved but you and I!"

Lying Words

Your lying words, sharp claws of birds of prey,
Your lips, as cold as the death,
I want you to stay.

March Winds

Finally, March is here,
Winds blow everything in their way,
The last snowmen slowly disappear,
The Spring is here, has come to stay.
I just got a new red kite,
My old friend, the wind, will help me with it to play,
I want to fly it to the highest height,
The Red Dragon, my new kite, the whole day.
My dog Cooper barked like crazy,
When he saw The Red Dragon up in the sky,
My eyes suddenly got hazy,
And I started to scream and cry.
The Red Dragon has just died in battle,
Tossed and shaken by my friend, the wind,
We lost the Kingdom we lost the Castle,
Only Cooper happy barks, following me close behind.

Marriage Proposal

It was a beautiful day, the end of May,
Her cheeks were red, like poppy flowers,
Full of emotions, trembling, I prepared the way,
And the few seconds then seemed like hours.
I didn't have a diamond ring,
I was a poor boy, as you guess,
Down on my knees, on that blessed spring,
I asked for her heart, and she said Yes.
Her smile struck a chord in me,
A song of Hallelujah was instantly born,
We'll tie the knot, but I feel free,
We are engaged! I blew my horn.
It was a beautiful day, the end of May,
That started our journey together here on earth,
Our hair is now at temples gray,
We shared the love we tasted its great worth.

Missing You

Oh, how I wish for you to be right here,
To wipe away my tears, to take away my fear,
So many longing songs unsung remain,
I wish I wish I wish in vain.
Too many mountain peaks are in my way,
What should I do, what should I say?
So many unquenchable tears of joy and pain,
So many sad dances danced in the rain.
So many ghosts still in my past,
My soul is sinking pretty fast,
So many dreams still to be dreamed,
Please, tell me can I be redeemed?
Frozen angels watch me crying,
The night it's dark, cold, terrifying,
Oh, how I wish for you to be right here,
To hold me tight, to keep you near.

Mom

You held me in your arms for the first time,
Warm tears were rolling down on your white cheeks,
And for the first time, I felt the love's delight,
I understood that this is how love speaks.
Drops of happiness betrayed your infinite excitement,
Our two hearts as one then began to beat,
entering in a new stage of love's enlightenment,
Your smile was angelic, and your breath so sweet.
So many sick days you watched over me,
Whispering with love, "You'll be fine!"
So many late nights spent on your knee,
You taught me love's reason to shine.
You were there with me when I took the first step,
You taught me when to move and when to stand still,
When to leave my worries on the doorstep,
You have inspired me with your power and your will.
You gave me comfort in pain and sorrow,
You were always by my side,
You taught me what's tomorrow,
You taught me how to read and how to write.
You walked with me on my first day of school,
The first book that we read together, it's now long past,
You taught me that to be myself is cool,
To live each day as the first one or maybe as the last.
With love and tender, you corrected all of my mistakes,
I still remember how you told me; You are the best!
No matter how much hurts or what it takes,
You always have to live the truth and stand the test.
You taught me to say what I think and what I feel,
Without any fear, always watching the sky,

To dream but also to know what is real,
To be powerful when I'm down and modest when I'm up high.
You taught me to comfort others with my love,
And to spread the Light, all around me,
You told me that I am a child of God's above,
You taught me to believe in Eternity!
So many precious things you planted in my heart,
You gave me life and taught me how to live it too,
You're up in Heaven, but we'll never be apart,
Today, tomorrow, always Mother, I Love You.

Moody Teenagers Are Like April

Moody teenagers are like April,
and April is like any moody teenager,
Today they're happy like a pretty, blossomed flower,
Tomorrow is happening something major,
They're angry, cold like the coldest shower.
You have to be always en garde
Be careful how you act around this fella,
But do not worry, it shouldn't be so hard,
If you carry with you a big umbrella.
You are protected if it's sunny or a rainy day,
Just think of them as of April,
Soon the moody month will go away,
(Your teenagers are growing way too fast),
So love them and be grateful.

Music palindrome

sound of angels flying-free
hearts covering light liberated
tears in happiness, tenderness of touch
love whispering
soul vibrating harmoniously
emotion-driven
-music-
driven-emotion
harmoniously vibrating soul
whispering love
touch of tenderness, happiness in tears
liberated light covering hearts
free-flying angels of sound

My Beautiful Angel

I pour love's pure nard every morning on your bare feet,
I kiss the sole of your foot.
The earth is wondering why are you limping?
It does not know that you walk like this fearing to crush my kiss.
I count the stars in your shining chestnut hair,
and the sky is envy at my blessings,
I carry your perfume and your smiles with me everywhere,
and the wind dreams of spring,
I am dazzled by the brightness of your fiery eyes,
and the sun is angry at my fortune.
I hug your glowing soul I hold your gentle heart,
You are mine, and heaven is jealous of my beautiful angel.

My Cute Bunny

My cute little white bunny,
together we will have a blast,
We will win a lot of money,
Who can run like you... so fast?
In the neighborhood's sprint game,
With all my friends, girls and boys,
We will make the Hall of Fame,
And we'll buy all the pretty toys.
With your tail just a small fluff
and your tiny, tiny paws,
I don't think, will be too tough
to be crowned with applause.

My Epitaph

I loved, I laughed, I cried
I felt the ocean, watched the sky
I'm happy on The Other Side
Because I live, I did not die.

My Frozen Butt

It's Winter in Chicago, once again,
Just a little bit of snow, that's no big deal,
Walls of eight-nine feet or ten
It's protecting us from the -25F wind to feel.
Today's traffic was a wreck.
Looking at downtown's majestic towers
I forgot about the snow up to my neck,
and those shoveling hours and hours.
I love my city, and I know I'm biased,
I always will, no matter what,
I don't care about my arthritis,
Nor about my frozen butt.
I'm brave enough to stick around,
I could never leave you Chicago, my dear,
I'm stuck with you like ice to ground,
I love you more each passing year.

My Love (QAP 8X10)

Why is the sky so clear and blue?
It's pure like my true love for you.
Why is the sun so burning hot?
It's to remind me what I got.
What did you get, if you don't mind?
I got my love, one of a kind.
Why is your love so special why?
She is the apple of my eye.
What is the name of your loved one?
It is a secret, but she's Ann.

"QAP 8X10" or "QAP 10X8", new forms created by Marius Alexandru, on February 2021 consists of 4-5 stanzas of 2 lines each stanza in a Question-Answer format.
QAP 8X10 form consists of 8 syllables each line with a total of 10 lines, respective 5 stanzas of 2 lines each.
QAP 10X8 form consists of 10 syllables each line with a total of 8 lines, respective 4 stanzas of 2 lines each.
It is a rhyming form with an AA BB CC DD EE rhyming scheme.
Both forms have 80 syllables, and are Question/Answer Style poems.
(first line the question second line the answer)
The name of the new form is "QAP" meaning Question Answer Poem.

My Puppy

I have a big bone for my puppy
I show it to him and his happy
He is wiggling his small tail
Following me on our daily trail
He's playing with the bone for hours
Eating all my grandma's flowers
Little puppy, what are you doing?
Now the garden is in ruin.
Next time, please, eat just the bone,
Until the new flowers will be grown.

My Soul is Sad

My soul is sad and cold.
Please, touch me with the fire of first Love,
to burn in my chest as before,
to spread The Love all around!

My wish is...

"One day, little Timmy saw a beautiful butterfly. In its silken wings, it
carried every color imaginable. The colors radiated in his eyes as he
approached the beautiful creature.
He took off his baseball cap, bowed, and said; I love you and honor
your greatness.
The butterfly, in turn, fluttered its wings and said; You are kind and
compassionate so I offer you a wish.
Little Timmy jumped for joy with the prospect of a wish. He sat on a
rock and pondering when suddenly he jumped up. "I got it I got it. My
wish is........"
from now on, on every winter to snow with stars
and sugar candies, said happy little, Timmy
I want a world with no more wars,
and all the kids to be like you, so pretty,
to have beautiful colors on our skin,
and to be able all to fly,
I want a world without sin,
I want forever just blue sky.
Stop, stop, I told you just one wish,
The smiling butterfly said,
Then, just to be like you, I guess
said Timmy, turning in his bed,
and he woke-up from his mysterious dream,
looking around for butterflies and stars,
they disappeared in the night, it seems,
Outside, just people walking in the snow and... cars.
Early in the morning, Timmy went to school
thinking of his dream and wish,
He stopped a minute by the neighbor's pool
Where he saw a beautiful creature, a multicolored fish.

He took off his baseball cap, bowed, and said. I love you and honor your greatness.

The fish, in turn, jumped with joy and said; You are kind and compassionate so I offer you a wish.

Little Timmy jumped for joy with the prospect of a wish. He sat on a rock and pondering when suddenly he jumped up. "I got it I got it. My wish is..."

No Barrier for Our Love

This world will never be strong enough,
To put a barrier for our love,
It might be hard it might be rough,
We'll conquer all the scary stuff,
All the darker clouds above.
When I am with you,
When I see your smiles when I see your tears,
All of my skies are clear and blue,
It's daily like my first "I do"
I am full of hope my fear disappears,
When in my dreams,
I can hear your voice, your laughter,
I'm deaf to all world's screams,
I walk with you beneath the trees, beside the streams,
A thousand years before, a thousand years after.
I'm not afraid of the passing time,
I'm not afraid of shadows,
I pour my love in every rhyme,
There are no mountains we can't climb,
I believe in colors I believe in rainbows.
I would never hurt you,
When I saw your smiles when I saw your tears,
From the first day, I met you I knew,
That what I feel is real and true
We'll fly together another thousand years.

No more Prison

Slowly the clouds dissipated in the skies,
A tear of joy in my eyes,
The stone fell on the side, no more prison,
Christ is alive! Christ has risen!

November

Rusty and golden leaves
fall on our silver and tired temples.
The woven of light falls apart
through the gray, heavy clouds.
November.

O silent night, O holy night, O night divine!

A silent night. It was a long, long silent night.
The hopes and dreams were lost for many years.
The sin's chains kept the cages full.
The wings were broken, nobody could fly,
The prophecies were forgotten, with no freedom in the sight.
O silent night, O holy night,
The hope is shining over the lost world, again.
The stars, filled with wonder,
join the angels clothed in light,
and sing a majestic song together.
At the break of dawn, at the edge of the village,
a Savior is born and laid in a manger.
O silent night, O holy night,
The King of Kings, a humble birth
Goodwill to men and peace on Earth!
Knees of clay pray in silence,
We bring gifts to the newborn King,
On the love's altar, the hearts are burning,
The souls grow wings and fly to kiss the heavens.
It snows slowly with flakes of blessings over the Earth,
The smiling Child has secretly given me a star.
I keep it forever in my heart to remind me of this Christmas Night.
It is mine. It shines, and it shines...
O silent night, O holy night, O night divine!
Over the World in Silence

Over the world in silence

It started to snow again,
with mystery stars,
of comfort and relief,
flakes of love and grace.
Heavenly voices are heard,
White angels caroling,
Their divine melody,
smoothly runs through the light
today, on this Christmas Day.
Quiet in the manger, Jesus
sleeps among the sheep,
The King from above,
has brought us joy,
Emanuel, God with us.
I wanted to see Him up close,
Full of peace, He smiles at me,
I shed a tear from my eyelids,
I fell on my knees and felt... agape,
God who loves me.
Over the world in silence,
The Child's cry resounds,
A divine breath,
breaking barriers forever,
Announcing once again the Good News.

Play for me

The Old Fiddler
Please play for me one of your songs,
The strings to cry in your hands,
I have no gold, I'll give you wine,
My coat and all that's mine.
Please play for me one of your songs,
Please use your old guitar,
Old fiddler please, I want to hear,
The music through my tear.
Please play for me, play from your heart,
The story of my love,
To shoot my longing for a day,
and happy fly away.
Please let me stay next to my cup,
To drink my pain, my sorrow,
I have no home I have no friends,
Today my journey ends.
Please let me stay in this dark pub,
To hear the silence crying,
To drink, to cry, but no regret,
My love, I won't forget.
Marius Alexandru, free translation "Sa-mi canti cobzar"

Playing with The Clouds

Fluffy clouds appear out of the blue,
It's raining with lights and flowers,
Looking for Cooper, I lost my magic shoe,
In these powerful Spring showers.
The gray clouds want to play,
Throwing thunders and lightning at us,
Scared Cooper run away,
Making such a big, unnecessary fuss.
I throwback at them my ball,
Hoping they will catch it and run,
When I heard my mama's call,
-Come inside the lunch is done.
-Two more minutes... here's the rainbow,
My dog happy is wagging his tail,
-Come on Cooper it's time to go,
He loudly barks and wail.

Poet's Interview (QAP 8X10)

What do you think poetry is?
A love story, a touch of bliss.
Why do you write? What mean to you?
It's like a cure my life shines through.
How did it change you? Tell us now?
I am a better man, somehow.
What if you'll never write again?
I think I'll cry lost in the rain.
How do you write? What's your secret?
Every word with love, I feed it.

"QAP 8X10" or "QAP 10X8", new forms created by Marius Alexandru, on February 2021 consists of 4-5 stanzas of 2 lines each stanza in a Question-Answer format.
QAP 8X10 form consists of 8 syllables each line with a total of 10 lines, respective 5 stanzas of 2 lines each.
QAP 10X8 form consists of 10 syllables each line with a total of 8 lines, respective 4 stanzas of 2 lines each.
It is a rhyming form with an AA BB CC DD EE rhyming scheme.
Both forms have 80 syllables, and are Question/Answer Style poems.
(first line the question second line the answer)
The name of the new form is "QAP" meaning Question Answer Poem.

Poetry is a reflection of thoughts

Poetry is a reflection of thoughts,
The writer's thoughts,
Reader's thoughts,
A mirror of ideas,
A portal to the imagination,
A breath of love, a flight, a dance,
It is an art that binds us together
in reality and beyond,
It is the color that fills our souls with beauty,
The key to understanding the mysteries of life,
Poetry is life itself.

Prayer

My knees of clay pray in silence,
In a corner, in my room,
Asking for Your strength, and guidance
For Your Light to light the gloom.
My heart is burning on this altar,
May my sacrifice be a pleasing aroma to You Lord,
Please, answer me, don't let me falter,
Don't let me be without reward.
My prayer gets before The Throne,
And worships inundated with Love,
Down, in the humble room, His presence shone,
The earth has met heaven above.

Prison for the Free-Haiku

tears pour down on walls
unfulfilled dreams, broken wings
prison for the free

Quotes by Marius Alexandru

the blessing is a mirror of giving
sometimes when the soul can no longer be silent it begins to write

Silence-Haiku

unheard music notes
deaf man dancing in the rain
silence at its best

Sing to me, old fiddler

Sing, sing to me, old fiddler
Let the strings cry under your hand of grace,
My soul is sad the night is bitter,
Put a smile in my sorrowful face.
Sing, sing to me, old fiddler
Change my pain in tears of joy,
The love has caught me, it holds me, prisoner
Under its spell, I'm just a boy.
Sing, sing to me, old fiddler
To soothe my longing for just a day,
My life is puzzled, I'm the Riddler,
Give me wings to fly away.
Sing, sing to me, more gracious than ever,
Let the stars dance to your tune,
Let the blue skies cry forever,
when the ocean touches the moon.

Singing Nightingales-Haiku

singing nightingales
green crowned hairstreak butterflies-
love story at night
Splashes of Colors-Haiku

Splashes of Colors

free spirit kissing the light
charming youthfulness

Spring Has Come

You opened the palm of your hand
and released the Spring.
The flowers gather in their petals
goldenrod variation, flamingo palettes,
brilliant colors and sweet perfume.
The garden's pathway is crowned with
bloom branches that blossom in the red sun.
Turquois butterflies fly, new wings are stained with vivid cadmium
yellow.
You sneak through murmuring spring's water
and dance with the rustle of the chrome wood forests.
You gathered in your eyes the whole universe,
and the time has stopped to smile
through the stars that embraced us.
You kissed me with spring on my old wintry eyelashes
and taught me what it means to love.

Spring's Victory

Blue butterflies dancing with me,
Old stars come down to kiss the earth,
The happy birds are flying free,
A time for perfume, endless mirth
New silver bells ring... Victory!
Snowdrops announce the new Spring birth.
Cherry blossom rise in splendor,
As the winter slow surrender!

Spring Starflower

I hide the last snow deep in my soul,
hoping to keep it there, safe,
until the next winter,
away from the sun baptism,
away from spring.
I am selfish.
I want to keep it just for me,
but she's free,
she belongs to heaven.
With one last look,
it smiles at me,
and full of love melts in the warmth of my soul,
becomes a drop of hope,
blossoming the beautiful white star,
the spring starflower.

Springs of Memories

So many longing songs remain unsung,
The mountains peaks still cry in the distance,
A complete silence spreads over the now-forgotten villages,
The springs of memories are reborn,
So many night stories remain untold,
Tears of joy and pain unquenchable
on the time's altar.

Tango

A dance descended from the light,
A sweet fragrance of pure joy,
Pains scattered in sounds at night,
Tango- the love's deliberate decoy.
It's not just dance, it's so much more,
It's two souls holding tight to each other,
Hermosa señora y hermoso senor,
Moving graciously together.
Tango, what a sweet fragrance!
Spread around the life's dance floor,
Where all emotions are pure and sacred,
Hermosa señora y hermoso senor.
Tango, what exquisite scent!
Felt in the kisses, in the crimson burning lips,
A happy, memorable event,
Delicate, deliberate love's sips.
One with the music, one with your dance partner,
Like the waves are one with the shore,
An innocent glance at that inner parlor,
Hermosa señora y hermoso senor.

Thank you

Thank You for being with me through the storms,
and You put a rainbow in the sky,
Your Will is always good.
Thank You for the sunny mornings,
When the rays caress me tenderly,
Thank You that You are my peace and comfort,
Thank You for the rain of blessings.

Thankful

Today I am so glad,
I'm thankful for mom and dad,
for their patience, love, and care,
for my little teddy bear,
my sister, my brother,
grandpa, grandmother,
friends from the old school,
Zeus, my dog... he's cool!
God knows that it's true,
I'm thankful for all of you.

Thanksgiving Prayer

The angel's songs vibrate in the strings of the violin,
and a tear descends trembling in the dusk,
So many questions are lost on the celestial paths,
But the thanksgiving prayer rises high, above all.
The silver trumpet sounds
when the prayer knocks to the Gate of Eternity,
Down on Earth, today, the world is better,
Faith was re-kindled.
The prayer gets before the Throne of Grace,
It worships overwhelmed with Love,
Lays down as a holy sacrifice on the altar,
and it burns incessantly in immortality.

That First Kiss

Holding out that little longer
Something special worth the wait
Noticed, meeting, crushing, dating
Then, at last, that first great kiss
It was a Spring day, end of May,
Her cheeks were red, like poppy flowers,
I whispered slowly, scared, please stay,
I hold her hand and talked for hours,
Holding out that little longer,
A blessed life, I happily say
Our genuine love becomes much stronger,
It was that first great kiss that made us stay.

The Autumn of My Life

The rusty light scatters in the rising winds,
Hills and valleys clothed in gold are smiling,
The crazy leaves are dancing as they lost their minds,
Over the orchards and vineyards, birds are flying.
The perfume from the winepress intoxicates me,
And it lifts me on the shore of dreams,
My whole being, stained by love shouts I'm free,
Flames, poems and songs overflow from my chest in streams.
Rains of happiness blossomed in my heart,
And in the autumn of my life, it's spring again,
The dry branches watered by love have a new start,
I'm a new man I'm a new man!
The earth got dirty with small drops of stars,
The fall's living carpet has laid,
I walk toward eternity forgetting all my scars,
The colors of the flower slowly fade.
A tear descends from the eyelash of a cloud,
A ray of hope to the groaning valley,
The heavens watch me, I am proud
as I approach The Grand Finale.

The Cave

Suspended between earth and heaven, I'm dreaming of ghosts,
I'm waiting in the dark, left to slowly burn alive
in the fire of the lost love,
Your love still cuts like a bloody knife,
Suspended between heaven and earth, I'm dreaming of heavenly hosts.
I hear the silence talking to the paintings on the walls,
The fire is long gone in the cave of the "Great Barrier"
It is so cold inside my soul,
I thought the end would be much scarier,
I hear the silence singing as the intolerable music falls.
The silver thimble around my neck shines
like a beacon of your eternal love,
The fine dry sand invades my immortal being,
I fly away, a free white dove,
Outside, concerned, continuously, the wind still whines.

The City of Love

My address is 777 NE-SW Hope Street, City of Love, Earth.
The second house on the right,
with the gate of red roses always open,
I lived here for as long as I remember, from my birth,
The old floors kissed the barefoot sole of my steps,
and the old walls are still echoing my first words that I have spoken.
On my street, all the people are laughing and smile,
And instead of "How are you?" everybody's saying; "I love You"
The City is surrounded by gardens, mile after mile,
and butterflies and flowers,
The sky above my City is always blue.
Every night the stars are dancing,
and the moon is telling stories to the kids,
The wind kisses the trees leaves singing and romancing,
In the City of Love, all the people have wings.
When it rains, it rains with dandelions and poppy flowers,
When it snows, it snows with daisies and snowdrops
In the City of Love, there's no time, no days nor hours,
In the City of love are infinite fields of cotton crops.
If you want to be my neighbor, you can move right next to me,
In the City of Love, we have places... plenty of,
With the view of the mountains or with the view of the sea,
There's no special requirement, come and see,
Just a simple one; to love.

.

The Death of The Deer

The drought has killed the wind's last breath,
The melted sun flowed on the earth facing its death,
The sky is hot, empty, and void,
The old wells full of mud, destroyed,
The forest is suffering, so many fires,
dancing with diabolical desires.
I follow my father up on the hill,
The evil pine trees cut deep wounds causing me pains,
Together, we go silently to hunt our deer,
The hunt of starvation in the Carpathian Mountains.
The thirst shatters me. The drips of water
are boiling on the rock.
My temple is pressing on my shoulder.
On a new, huge, heavy,
on the unknown planet, I walk.
We're waiting in a place where the springs are still singing,
With their smooth, magical strings to the ear,
By dusk, moon and silence clinging,
Here will come in droves, to drink, one by one the deer.
I tell my father I'm thirsty, beckons me to shut up,
Oh, dizzying water, the clearest one I saw,
I feel thirst-bound to you. You're condemned to death
by rules, traditions, and by the natural law.
The valley breathes with a faint rustle.
What a terrible evening floats in the universe!
The blood is flowing in the horizon, and my chest is red
as if I wiped my bloody hand on it from this curse.
Ferns burn with purple flames, I can see the altar, I can hear the drum,
Even some astonished stars blinking are crying,
How much I wish that you would not come, you would not come,

The beautiful offering of my forest, you are dying!
She jumped up, and then stood still,
She fearfully gazed around for a moment,
Her thin nostrils made the water thrill
in a rusty circling movement.
I saw in her wet eyes confusion,
I knew that she would suffer, that her death is near,
It was like reliving a myth, a wild dream, an illusion,
The story about the girl turned into a deer.
From above, the pale lunar light
sifted cherry blossoms on her warm fur,
Ah, how I wished that for the first time that night,
the bullet from my father riffle to miss the target, to miss her!
Suddenly, the valleys roared. Kneeling,
she raised her head and shook it to the stars,
Then she collapsed stirring
black swarms of beads on the water, her scars.
A bluebird, from the branches, is flying free from all,
The life of the sweet deer toward the eternal rest
it had flown, screaming like a bird, leaving in the fall
her empty, dry, deserted nest.
Stumbling, I closed her shady, sadly eyes
guarded by her horns somehow discreet,
I winced silently, vivid like a ghost when my father
proudly shouted: We have meat!
I tell my father I'm thirsty, beckons me to drink,
Oh, dizzying water, the darkest one I saw,
I feel thirst-bound to you. You are already dead
because of rules, traditions, and because of the natural law.
The law is useless, full of shades,
When life in us so quickly fades,
Traditions and mercies are just echoes flying,

When my sister is hungry, sick, and dying.
The smoke is coming silently from my father's gun,
Without any wind, the scared leaves wildly run and run!
My father makes a frightening fire,
The forest trees sing in the saddest choir!
I catch from herbs, unknowingly, and I cannot tell,
a little silver tinkling bell.
With his bare hands, out of the skewer, dad had set apart
the deer's kidneys and her roasted heart.
What's your problem, heart? I'm hungry! I want to live, to conquer
fear!
Please forgive me, virgin, maiden, my beautiful deer!
I'm sleepy. How high is the fire! I hear the forest beat!
I cry. What is my father thinking? I eat and cry. I eat!
Marius Alexandru
free translation of the poem "Moartea Caprioarei" de Nicolae Labis

The Evening on The Hill

The horn is mourning on the hill, in the new evening,
The herds slowly climb it, the stars show the way, happy shining,
The waters weep into the wells, clearly springing,
Under an acacia tree, you, my darling, are waiting.
Holy and clear the moon pass through the skies,
You, scout through the leaves with your very bright eyes,
The stars give birth, on the sky with clear nights,
Your heart is filled with longings, your mind filled with thoughts.
Rushing clouds fight with the sunrays at noon,
Old hidden houses dance under the full moon,
Broken and rusty well's bucket squeak in the wind,
The valley is in a fog, the murmuring whistles left behind.
Weary peasants with their scythes on their back
Return from the fields; tired but happy they walk the same track,
The old bell fills with the sound, the new evening,
My soul full of your love is slowly burning.
Ah!, soon, very soon the village in the valley will be silent,
The sound of my steps, in a hurry to you, can be heard in this quiet,
By the acacia tree, we will sit hours, the whole night,
Declaring our love for each other until the morning's first light.
We finally will be sleeping. You, with your beautiful head on my chest,
I, dreaming of how fortunate I am, and how blessed,
The old acacia and the moon are watching over us from the sky,
For a night like this, who wouldn't be willing to die?

free translation of "Sara pe Deal" Mihai Eminescu

Flame of My Hope

The flame of my hope,
even if sometimes it barely burns,
lights in me a bright, shining fire,
The heat and light it emits increases,
reminds me that I'm immortal.
Touch me with the fire of first Love,
to burn in my chest as before,
to spread The Love around!

The Hippo Ballerina-Limerick

On the greatest dance world's arena
I'm the happiest ballerina
I float like a snowflake
A pink "swan" on the lake
Raised by Pablo in Argentina

The Hope is Regained

The suffering covers us like black gloves,
Love and faith are tied to a concrete pole
with chains of fear and despair.
The storm is too strong. The night is too long.
The boat is drifting. The sun is hiding.
The winds loudly howl. The wolves, in the forest, growl.
There is no future, no proper scope, there is no hope.
But He took off our gloves. He shared our suffering.
He broke all the chains.
He freed the love. He freed the faith. No more fear!
The storm is gone. The day has come.
The sun is shining. The boat is peacefully sailing.
The winds are singing. The forest is dancing.
We have a future, a final aim. The hope is regained.

The Last Season

We buried so many autumns together,
and so many dead leaves are hiding in the sunset of our lives,
We kissed so many stars on the clear nights,
The waves have dug in the rock so many pains,
so many traces, so many tears.
We are slowly heading for the last season.
So many raindrops are hanging behind our eyelids,
ready to dance with the longings that burn in our chest,
So many answered prayers lay their petals on the holy water,
We feel You at the door, God, You are so close!
Ah, Lord, we are waiting for You!
Songs of joy, songs of thanksgiving resound in the violin strings,
and in the verses of poetry,
Grace covers us,
The clay has startled, wrapped in warm shivers,
It smells like spring, the flowers bloom again,
Not far away, in the silence of the night, we can hear the shofar.

The Leaf and The Earth

I am a golden, fallen leaf,
happy to kiss the sole of your barefoot,
I am a subtle, pretty thief,
I will lay there I'll stay put,
I bathed your eyes in beauty,
I vanished, to be born in the love I have for you,
I am a hot redheaded cutie,
In love with your hair greys blue.

....

I am the dry, thirsty earth,
happy to take your kisses and hide them inside me,
Precious seeds to immortal mirth,
busting out and getting free.
The woven of light
falls apart through the gray, heavy clouds,
Prepared to say good night
on a corner of the sky, a star makes its nest away from crowds.
Dying little by little,
we are advancing towards Life,
under the spell of the forest's whistle,
the leaf and the earth, a husband and a wife.

The Magical Window

I woke up in the middle of the night,
I saw through my window stars playing with a kite,
I saw the moon smiling, throwing kisses at me,
I want to play with them, so I went down slowly,
jumping from tree to tree.
I played for many days with butterflies and birds,
I listened to angels' choirs and fairies' whispers, magic words,
I danced with flowers and played hide and seek with bunnies,
I ate from the hand of a friendly, little bear, the sweetest honey.
I swam in a pool full of gold,
I was told that if you swim there, you'll never get old,
I flew with seagulls, over the ocean, toward the sun,
I saw many planets I had so much fun.
I woke up in the morning all joyful and happy,
I looked at my window the sun was smiling at me,
A new day, full of adventures I realized has just begun,
So many windows to open, so many magic lands to play and to run.

The Nicest Walrus at the Zoo (Double Limerick)

I am the nicest walrus at the zoo,
If you know me, you'll agree with me too,
All I want is a small kiss,
My old friend, I surely miss,
So, just for now, your pretty face should do.
Our great love lasts forever never ends,
We destined for each other, why pretends
that we are two strangers here?
Can't you see? I love you, dear.
For you, I'll give up fish, will make amends.

It's The Faces I Remember Jerry Jeff Walker October 2020
"I've lost so many friends now
my life seems like a dream
all the things we did with joy
and all that laughter in between
the times that we were rascals
and the poetry we shared
they said our heads were in the clouds
but I said our hearts were everywhere"

The Old Faces

Your time on earth was not enough
to dance and write and sing,
From your short dream, you just woke up,
to a New Life, Eternal Spring.
You got to meet your friends again,
The old faces with their laughter and their smiles,
You'll walk together through the stars, dancing in the rain,
a million years, a million miles,
with your guitar and cowboy hat,
playing for angels your new song,
(a new-old star is born... imagine that!)
and all your friends playing along.
11/05/2020

The Silence

Touching with one finger her lips, the moon signals me to shut up.
Quietly I listen to her urge, and I am overwhelmed by the silence's
whispers.
I look at my window.
It is covered with millions of stars that send me infinite kisses from
above.
I fell asleep in peace, dreaming of happy angels that guard silently, my
sleep.

The Silent Village in The Valley

On the hill,
the horn is no longer mourning in the evening,
The stars
drown in smoke, and the sheepfolds are all empty.
The waters weep the turmoil left in the fountains,
Even the old acacia forgot about me.
The moon,
in the sky stopped dazed,
You walk among the leaves
lost,
The stars die buried in a cloud,
There is no room for longing in your cold chest.
The rushing clouds
prevailed at noon,
Hidden houses dance under the full moon,
The fountain bucket has been broken for a long time,
The valley is in a fog, and I don't hear any whistles anymore.
Today,
no one goes to the scythe,
No one cares about the weeds in the field anymore,
No more bells ringing in the evening,
My soul is no longer burning with expectation.
Ah! the village
in the valley has long been silent,
Ah! my step towards you is not in a hurry,
Acacia!
Ah! the old acacia is cut,
and we almost forgot the love.
I don't even remember your face,
Your cold eyes sink slowly into a hole,

My head heavy falls on the old acacia,
God, what are we doing now?
God, what are we going to do now?

The Spring of 2020

The wind blows in the deserted streets,
and a sad song whistled lightly
filled with terror, the joy on earth retreats,
shocked by this great tragedy.
It's a dark and ugly Spring,
All the flowers forgot to bloom,
I cannot hear the robin sing,
Everything smells of stale perfume.
Death walks slowly through the hospitals
and the doomed are taking hold of her hand,
It makes me feel so powerless, so little
Please forgive us, Father, heal the land.
The children stay at home (there is no school)
not understanding why they cannot see their grandparents,
We all wear masks, and we follow the new rule
when walk outside running some errands.
Today, millions and millions of people,
raise their weeping eyes to the sky again,
looking for answers, looking for a reason,
Praying for blessings, for forgiveness's rain.
Under the masks, we hide our old-fashioned smile,
as our hugs slowly, slowly fade,
We hope that heaven and earth can reconcile,
We put our lives on the scale to trade.
Let the rainbow appear once more,
Receive our prayer and repentance
Get rid of the terrible storm, show us the shore,
Forgive us what is left of our sentence.
I can see through the leaves how a new petal is born,
Through the flowering trees, the birds sing a song,

I dream of the blessed, glorious morn',
I know, He's at the door, He's coming it won't be long!

The Sweet Flavor of Love's Fruit

I had some butterfly in my stomach,
At the thought of holding her by hand,
I saw her from the distance coming,
Until today I cannot understand,
How could she like a kid like me,
I smelled her hair, and felt her breath,
I hid fast my bruised knee,
And waited patiently for my "death".
It was a Spring day, end of May,
Her cheeks were red like poppy flowers,
I whispered slowly, scared, please stay,
I hold her hand and talked for hours.
I sipped her words that flew like birds,
I dreamt of making her to stop,
I wished my words to touch her words,
Together dripping drop by drop.
I finally took courage, I was bold,
For a split second she was mute,
I think I was five years old,
I tasted the sweet flavor of love's fruit.
(a poem on my first kiss, WITHOUT using the words—kiss, lips,
mouth, and tongue)

The White Swan-Haiku

kiss the lake at dawn
graceful, divine, majestic
new queen, the white swan

The Woman Without Name

Tied in heavy chains of pain,
The flame of faith slowly goes out,
So many fights she fought in vain,
Her tired soul is full of doubt.
So many questions with no answers,
All dreams and hopes begin to fade,
She thought she took all given chances,
Her life's light darkens, shade by shade.
There is a little courage left,
A mustard seed faith in her heart,
She's ready to commit the theft,
A touch by faith and a new start!
My trembling hand searching for You,
So many feet are hurting me,
I see Your cloak, If I get through,
A simple touch, and I'll be free.
I do not care about the crowds,
I do not care for their accusing eyes,
There is a rainbow, no more clouds,
The sun is smiling in the skies.

The World, a Wonderful Picture

I can see the beauty in the sunrise,
In the breeze, in the ocean's whispers,
In the smile of a child, in his beautiful eyes,
In all the trees dancing along the rivers.
I can feel the love in every hug, in every kiss,
Your candid look, your gentle touch
fills my soul with joy and bliss.
I enjoy life, is this too much?
I can hear music, angel choirs,
Birds singing in the forests and mountains,
The sunset crying in seraphic fires,
Torrents of blessings from the old fountains.
I can taste the goodness of this wonderful world,
Full of faith and hope, I can see the bright future,
I refuse to be drawn to fear and to be hurled,
With colors of love, I paint the world, a wonderful picture.

Touch my Soul with Your Fatherly Hand

Untie the rope of my old nature Lord,
and break the heavy chains of sin and burden,
Clothe me with the robe of faith,
and set my footsteps on the path of happiness,
towards the eternal Spring.
Open my eyes and let me see,
Help my unbelief, give me strength,
like the white snowdrop, raising from under the snow,
at the arm with the flowers in a holy crusade,
to always fly, cheerfully to the Resurrection!
Touch my soul with Your Fatherly Hand,
and fill my heart with joy,
Never to be disturbed again,
and for You daily, she tenderly to beat,
with love and longing for Eternity.

Trust

Sometimes the worry's mountains
are standing right in front of me,
Oh, how I want a faith that moves them,
Oh, how I want to be like Thee!
Your Ways are always higher than my own,
I trust Your Will, Your Voice, Your Time,
I know that You're here, I'm not alone,
The mountains in my life are here to teach me how to climb.
Your Thoughts are not my thoughts,
But I am resting in Your reassurance,
And when I feel my soul tied up in many knots,
I know You want to teach me patience and endurance.
Sometimes the fear's storms are all around me,
Oh, how I want to see the end of the night,
I know; Your Voice can silence any storm sea,
I trust in You, and I know; You are The Light.

Valentine's Day Sonnet

Oh, how you stole my heart with your great smile,
I couldn't keep it anymore just for me,
From that moment, we walked mile after mile,
Chained together our hearts-one, flying free.
Oh, how you stole my heart with your first kiss,
And how my wings grew instant with your touch,
Your every touch felt like a touch of bliss,
I love you, my darling, so much, so much...
Oh, how you stole my heart with your whispers,
It was like angels singing from the sky,
So many years with laughter and with tears,
And many sun rays, many clouds passed by.
How did I steal your heart? Please tell me this,
It was my first smile, my first touch, first kiss?

Watching Over Me at Christmas

It's snowing beautifully outside
crystals are flying everywhere,
The streets are covered in bright white,
and love is in the air,
Frozen windows tremble
when happy carolers are passing by,
White angels, disguised in snowflakes
are dancing in the sky.
I'm snuggled up, all warm and cozy
by my fireplace, inside,
The sound of burning wood,
a melody so peacefully, so sublime,
I'm reading The Christmas Story,
by the candlelight,
A smiling star waving at me,
whispers good night, good night...
Crumbs of stars from above
sifts blessings over my house and my dreams,
Watching over me at Christmas, The Love
in heavenly splendor gleams.

We Wear a Mask

We wear a mask deep on our souls,
It tries to cover all the pain,
It tries to cool all burning coals,
It is a mask we wear in vain.
At life's carnival, we all dance,
We wear a mask and hide our smile,
We got caught in this old trance,
Bleeding hearts and subtle guile.
We wear a mask that hides our beauty,
Our tears are dry under its power,
It is a right? It is a duty?
We cannot breathe nor smell a flower.
We wear a mask, try to comply,
But without God, we will not stand,
We traded our life for a big lie,
We hide our heads in the dark sand.
The mask, it's now wearing our souls,
It tries to hide from us the pain,
We lost our meanings we lost our roles,
It is a mask we wear in vain.

We Wear a New Mask

The same old mask we wear again,
We didn't change why we pretend?
We wear a mask, but in our eyes
is fear, and hate, and lies.
The same old mask we wear again,
The face is covered, but the pain
that's planted deep in our souls
have left dark marks and open holes.
The same old mask we wear again,
We have our tears, we cry in vain,
We try to smile, but who can see?
Why we pretend that we are free?
We wear a mask, the same old mask,
We are afraid even to ask,
For how long God when this will end?
When I will hug again my friend?
We wear a mask, it's a new mask,
A new world order, a new task,
We wear a mask, but our songs
are flying free. The heart to You belongs.

We Will Heal Together in Love

I will borrow a part of your soul,
and like a piece of a puzzle, like a perfect match,
I will add it to the missing part of the center of my soul
to finally make it whole again.
Then, with my new soul,
I will cover the scar I did in yours,
and we will heal together in love.

What is Love, in the eyes of six years old child?

A kiss from my mom each night on my forehead,
A smile and a hug when I fall, from my dad,
Forgiveness from my brother when I play with his toy-car,
or from my sister when I eat the last candy from the jar,
A lick on my cheeks from Max, my new dog,
Miss Piggy, together with Kermit The Frog.
The hands of my grandfather throwing me up high,
The grandmother's pear compote or her sweet apple pie.
Lucas, my neighbor when he brings me his cat
Olivia, my cousin, letting me borrow her beautiful red hat.
The rain when we jump, just for fun, in the mud,
A soft blow on my scars, bandages for blood.

You Are My All

You make me smile through the dark clouds and rainy days.
You make me happy when I smell the coffee in the mornings.
You make me laugh when I hear your funny stories and we cried
together
at so many movies in the evenings.
You and only you know how to listen to my heartbeats and
understand
my unspoken words.
You wipe away the tears of my soul and tend to my broken wings.
You cover me with your blanket of love every night.
You are my blessing, my happiness, my life, my all.

Your counterfeited love burns like a real fire

If lying is a sin, then our love is heading straight to hell,
The way you lie is something that you learned in the old garden,
I'll rather spend my life with you in an eight-foot cell,
I'll rather be your cellmate than your warden.
Your lying words are like the sharp claws of birds of prey,
Your lips are as cold as the death to living creatures,
I love the way you lie. I want you here with me to stay,
I do not care about the heavens. I do not care about the future.
Your counterfeited love burns like a real fire,
I love the way you lie even if it hurting my whole heart,
You'll never be able to turn me into a liar,
I love you, and we'll never grow apart.
I'm sick. Right on my spine, I feel a chill,
I'm willingly chained to all your pretty lies,
A slave returning love for ill,
To all the lying words, I close my eyes.
What if I find the truth? What should I do with it?
What difference does it make to know?
I love your lies, and I admit,
I'll never want to let you go.
If lying is a sin, then our love is heading straight to hell,
I am an accomplice in deceit, not the executioner,
I love the way you lie. I love the way you tell me all is well,
I love the way your lie it holds me prisoner.

Your Smile

I dug deep into the root of a young tree,
and I hid your smile there,
I just wanted to keep it to myself,
away from the sad and evil world,
But I found it over the years,
in thousands of golden leaves,
who smiled discreetly at me in the sun.
I understood then that the world is more beautiful
thanks for your smile.
A leaf touched my lips and two smiles
they merged forever with the forest.

About the Author

Marius Alexandru born, and raised in Arad, Romania, came to the United States in 1997, where he currently lives with his wife.His passion for poetry started as a child, and he has been writing poetry since his adolescence.He is the author of a few Romanian Christian poetry books, including "Fosnetul Pasilor din Duzi", "Scaldati in Susurul Bland al Harului", "Doruri Sfinte", English Poetry "Ring of Fire-Poems", and many other poems in both Romanian and English languages.

Read more at https://www.resursecrestine.ro/poezii/index-autori/alexandru-marius/album/scaldati-in-susurul-bland-al-harului.